MW01089268

# The Jesse Tree
A Story of Unexpected Abundance

By Matt Timms

Illustrations by Sam Gutierrez

Download a PDF of all 24 symbols
to hang on your tree

granitesprings.org/jessetree

Hi,

This is a gift from Granite Springs Church. It's called **The Jesse Tree**. We began this project last spring as a way to bless our own congregation and some generous donors wanted to give full-time Jessup faculty a gift. So, here it is – a gift from us to you. If you already have an Advent practice that helps you draw more deeply into the story of God's faithful love, then please feel free to give this copy to a friend or neighbor, or save it until next year.

Written by Matt Timms, a Jessup employee and Worship Coordinator at Granite Springs Church and illustrated by Sam Gutierrez - Pastor of Spiritual Formation at Granite Springs – this version of the Jesse Tree is a modern approach to an ancient practice that will connect with both young and old in fresh ways. Inside the front cover is a link that you can follow to download PDF's of all the artwork to print, cut out and hang on your own tree at home. If you want more copies, you can order them from Amazon.

Enjoy and Merry Christmas!

Sam Gutierrez

*"This will surely be a Christmas grace to people of every age and spiritual experience. Take and read!"*

**Kevin Adams / Author of 150: Finding your story in the Psalms**

*"The Jesse Tree is a compelling and satisfying way to mark the days in anticipation of Christ's birth. When God's ageless story is told in this way, its beauty rings true for those who know it well and those hungry to learn it. You'll be blessed by the gifts of stillness and grace that lie within this book."*

**Aaron Antoon / Worship Leader at Granite Springs Church**

**www.granitesprings.org**

# What Is the Jesse Tree? An Introduction

> "A shoot will come up from the stump of Jesse;
> from his roots a Branch will bear fruit." (Isaiah 11:1)

For hundreds of years, people have drawn, painted, and sculpted Jesse Trees to depict the people in Jesus' family tree. In fact, some Jesse Tree art is over 500 years old!

Today, the Jesse Tree is usually a branch or tree on which we hang symbols that help us remember the stories of people in Jesus' family tree. The stories represented on the Jesse Tree aren't the only important stories, nor is every Jesse Tree the same, but they are some of the critical stories that tell of God's ongoing faithful action to come near to us.

The Jesse Tree is typically a 24-day practice that people can use to prepare for the celebration of Christ's birth at Christmas. It helps us enter more fully into the church season of Advent, which anticipates the coming of Jesus and is a season of expectation. The Jesse Tree provides us with a tangible way to count down and look toward Jesus' coming through the stories of the Old Testament. It's a great way to enter this season!

## The Images

The use of symbols to teach or to reflect on who God is and who we are has a long tradition in Christianity. St. Augustine (5th century) used the image of a pear tree to reflect on his own brokenness. Julian of Norwich (15th century) had a vision of a ball the size of a hazelnut that she used to meditate on God's care and love for his world. St. John of the Cross (16th century) depicted part of our spiritual journey as being like a dark night. Architects and artists used stained glass and carved stone in the great cathedrals to help teach illiterate Christians the stories of the Bible.

This version of the Jesse Tree tries to take some small steps into this image-rich tradition. Each day's reflection is not just a reiteration of the biblical story. Rather, it is an attempt to use images to explore more deeply the truth of God's story. Sam's simple, arresting, and beautiful artwork is there to help you along with that journey. The hope is that this approach will allow you (and whoever you might be exploring the Jesse Tree with) to meditate on and call to mind these stories in a visual way. Christians have been doing it for a long time, so why not join in?

## What to Look For

One of the fun things about writing and reflecting on these stories is that themes begin to come to the surface. While I am confident you will discover your own themes and connections (that would be a good thing to discuss with others!), I felt that two related themes were worth highlighting here, as they wind throughout most of these stories.

The first theme is that God seems to work in unexpected ways, ways that surprise us. Over and over again in these stories, God does something that is either undeserved or unexpected, using people in surprising ways or acting in ways that catch them off guard. It is beautiful and delightful to be reminded of the fact that the God of the Bible is one who loves surprises.

The second theme is that God loves to do things in abundance. He is not a God of quarters or halves. He does things all the way: loves, gives grace, acts faithfully towards us, comes close.

One or the other of these themes seems to wind through most of these stories, and it might be fun to see where they pop up in your reading and exploring. Ultimately, I think we see them coming together perfectly on Day 24, but hey, no spoilers!

## How to Use Your Jesse Tree

For the practically-minded and the direction-followers among us, the critical piece of using and practicing the Jesse Tree is just, well, to try to use it. Each day has a number of elements that you can engage with or skip; it is really up to you. If you miss a day, move on, or go back and make it up. The point is not to do every element, but to engage in the anticipation of Christ and enter more deeply into God's story in our own lives.

Each day contains a short-ish passage from Scripture (there is sometimes a longer asterisked passage in parentheses for those who want more), a summary, a reflection, questions for conversation/reflection, and a prayer. Pick and choose what works best for you and/or those you're reflecting with.

In the conversation questions, the first one is designed to be easier to answer and to bring children into the conversation. The second one can lead into a deeper conversation. That said, I've tried to write the reflections not just for families, but for anyone interested in a faith-based practice for this season. My hope is that it is as helpful for single people and empty-nesters as it is for people with children.

May God bless you richly on your Jesse Tree journey.

Matt Timms

# The Jesse Tree
A Story of Unexpected Abundance

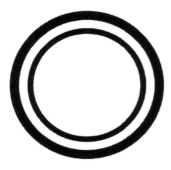

## Day 1

**Symbol:** The World
**Reading:** Genesis 1:1-2, 28-30 (Genesis 1:1-2:3*)
**Summary:** Today's symbol is the world. It's a reminder that in the beginning of our story, God got involved, created all things, and declared them to be good.

**Reflection:**
Have you ever seen pictures of the earth from space? Some say it looks like a giant blueberry. It's both big and small at the same time. You can see continents and oceans and feel the dizzying bigness of space. You can see light, wispy clouds, and big hurricanes. You can see it all in a snapshot. It looks beautiful. Isn't it a nice perspective? Perhaps this is even what we think God sees. God, floating out in space somewhere, looking from a distance at a big blueberry that he made.

But that's not what how the story actually goes.

In the second verse of the whole Bible, the idea of a distant God is shattered. There, the Spirit of God is hovering over the waters. God is already there, excited, expectant, perhaps even quivering with anticipation. It's the first "grace moment" in a story that is full of them. A God who could have just looked on comes close and creates. He makes light and land, plants and penguins, sun and seas. As he goes, this involved-God, this present-God, looks on and says "It is good."

That's the way we will see God work throughout his story. He doesn't work at a distance. He gets in the midst of things and gets his hands dirty. He shapes the entire creation until he looks at us, at humanity, and says "It is very good." And that's just the beginning.

## Questions:

1. What's your favorite thing to learn about or explore in God's good creation?
2. What would your life look like if you believed that God's words about the creation ("It is very good") were true of you personally?

## Prayer:

Creative Father,

Thank you that you made us. Thank you that you didn't stay at a distance but have come close to us and gotten involved, from the beginning and even now. Open our eyes to the creative ways you want to shape us and renew us. Make us more like you - compassionate and near, creative and good - as we engage with those around us. We pray this in the name of Jesus the Son, who dwells with you and the Holy Spirit: one God, now and forever, amen.

**Day 2**

**Symbol:** The Serpent and the Fruit
**Reading:** Genesis 3:1-7 (Genesis 3:1-19*)
**Summary:** Today's symbol is the serpent and the fruit. It's a reminder that, like our ancient parents, we lose our way and choose to disobey God and need his help to restore us.

**Reflection:**
Fruit can look so good. Fresh on the tree. In a commercial, with the lighting just right. Fruit can *sound* so good. The crunch of an apple. The pop of biting into a grape. And fruit *is* good. We are encouraged to eat multiple servings each day.

But fruit can also go bad. It can have worms and bruises. It can make your trash smell and invite the ants to come marching through your kitchen.

Where we tend to get into trouble is when we cannot tell whether fruit is good or bad. Today's symbol reminds us of that. The fruit in the story looked "good for food and pleasing to the eye" but it was being pitched by a crafty serpent who was interested not in a feast, but in upending God's desires.

Like our ancient parents, Adam and Eve, we too can get distracted by what we think is good fruit. We eat fruit that looks good but is actually rotten. We join in bullying the kid next door.

We do whatever it takes to get a promotion. After eating that rotten fruit, we find ourselves feeling empty and sick.

From the beginning of time, people have needed someone to teach us which fruit to eat and which to avoid. But we also need someone to heal us when we choose the rotten fruit. And from early in our story, God has had a plan to do just that through his Son, Jesus.

**Questions:**
1. What's something you have done that you later felt bad about doing?
2. Why do you think we get confused or struggle to determine what is good or what is bad? What clouds our judgment?

**Prayer:**
Healing Father,
Like our ancient parents, Adam and Eve, we find ourselves attracted to things that are bad for us; things that seem good at the time but rot in our souls. In your grace, and because of Jesus, we ask that you would redirect our desires. May we desire you more than the fruit that tempts us. In your grace, and because of Jesus, we ask that you would heal us. Reach into our areas of brokenness and make us whole, as you long for us to be. We pray this in the name of Jesus the Son, who dwells with you and the Holy Spirit: one God, now and forever, amen.

## Day 3

**Symbol:** The Ark and the Rainbow
**Reading:** Genesis 6:11-21, 7:17-8:1, 9:8-13 (Genesis 6:9-9:17*)
**Summary:** Today's symbol is the ark and the rainbow. These images remind us that God's character is deep: he makes things right in judgment *and* he delights in showing us grace.

### Reflection:

If you have ever seen floodwaters, they are not soothing. Floods are not some kind of big bath where the water is nice and clean and inviting. The waters are turbulent and muddy. They leave behind water damage and silt. The water is powerful and awesome in the literal sense—its power inspires awe.

Rainbows are something different. They come when light hits water droplets and gets spread out in the sky. These droplets create a beautiful range of colors such that you can't help but poke someone and say "Hey, look!"

Floodwaters. Rainbow waters. The same substance, two very different results.

The story of the flood reminds us of the depths of God. Like water, he can be powerful and awesome, and he can be gentle and captivating. In fact, he's both. In Genesis 6, humanity's constant choosing of the rotten fruit had filled the earth with violence, and our good God had to do something about it. So out pours his judgment, and the floodwaters cover the earth.

But God is also a gracious God. So in the midst of the turbulent waters he preserves Noah and his family and every kind of animal. In the end, entirely unprompted and undeserved, God promises Noah that despite what he or his descendants might do, God won't flood the earth again in that way.

We have a God of both floodwaters and rainbow waters. Isn't it amazing that God most often chooses the rainbow?

**Questions:**

1. Can you think of other things like water that can be both powerful and gentle in different forms?
2. How does the fact that God is simultaneously just and gracious impact the way you think about him or approach him?

**Prayer:**

Powerful Father, Gentle Father,

With Christians of all times and all places, we confess that you are beyond us. We struggle to understand how all these aspects of your character—your holiness and power, your gentleness and compassion—work perfectly together. Thank you for sending us Jesus, who embodies your character, that we might see and hear and follow. Help us be people who are marked by your character in such a way that it points to you. We pray this in the name of Jesus the Son, who dwells with you and the Holy Spirit: one God, now and forever, amen.

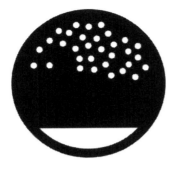

**Day 4**

**Symbol:** A Sky Full of Stars
**Reading:** Genesis 12:1-7, 15:1-7
**Summary:** Today's symbol is a sky full of stars. The sky full of stars reminds us of God's great promises to his people, and his deep faithfulness to keep them even when we might doubt that he is working.

**Reflection:**
It seems like the closer one gets to cities and their lights—traffic lights, stadium lights, house and apartment lights—the further one gets from stars. Sometimes it seems like you can count the stars you can see on one hand, and then you realize that one of them was an airplane. But when you're camping or on a farm, there are so many stars in the sky that you can't count them.

There's one point, however, when nobody sees the stars: during the day. It doesn't matter whether you live downtown or in the middle of nowhere, in the middle of the day you just can't spot the stars. They're still there, but they can't be seen.

God points to the stars as a sign of the abundant promise he gives to Abraham: the promise to make Abraham into a great nation. But, interestingly, this star-sign was only available on a part-time basis. We might wonder if sometimes, in the heat of the day, Abraham doubted that God was with him. Beyond his sight, the stars were still there and God was still working, but it could be hard to see.

Our faith journey is often the same. Sometimes God seems as clear as the stars in a dark night sky, and sometimes, for all our straining, we can't spot him at all. But, like the stars, God is always present. He is with us in our seasons of faith and in our seasons of doubt. God's faithfulness is part of his character, and Abraham's story reminds us that this is true whether we can see it or not.

## Questions:
1. Where have you seen an especially beautiful night sky?
2. What parts of God's character (his faithfulness, his goodness, his power, etc.) do you find it hardest to see evidence of? What would help you believe that those good characteristics are real, even without seeing them?

## Prayer:
Present Father,

When we are full of faith, you are with us. When we are full of doubts, you are with us. Thank you that regardless of our faith or lack thereof, you are faithful to your promises. Give us the eyes to see you at work in our life, that we might always be reminded of your promise to finish the good work you have started—a work to make us more like Jesus.

We pray this in the name of Jesus the Son, who dwells with you and the Holy Spirit: one God, now and forever, amen.

**Day 5**

**Symbol:** A Ram
**Reading:** Genesis 22:1-14 (Genesis 22:1-19*)
**Summary:** Today's symbol is a ram. The ram reminds us that God, in our seasons of struggle and intensity, longs to offer us relief.

### Reflection:

When you look at a sheep, what do you think? Maybe you visit a farm and you're curious—you don't always see farm animals up close, and a sheep's bleating sounds different in person than the "baa baa" of your childhood songs. Maybe you're driving a country road only to find sheep blocking the way and you're frustrated. Maybe you don't have any strong emotional reaction to a sheep (that's probably normal). But what if you encountered a sheep and experienced relief?

Today's story is one that Jews and Christians have puzzled over for thousands of years. At God's request (and to our puzzlement), Abraham and Isaac go to worship. God has asked Abraham to offer Isaac, his only son, to God as a sacrifice. In a moment filled with tension and a raised knife, God provides a ram to take Isaac's place. We can imagine Abraham's relief. He had a way out—a ram of relief.

Most of us are in desperate need of relief as well. We might not experience the extreme test that Abraham went through, but we find ourselves with pent-up stress or worry or pain. Relief sounds great, but it seems so far away.

But Abraham's story points to another story that happened a long time after. It points to God coming to us in Jesus. It points to Jesus sacrificing himself in our place so that we might take a full breath, free from sin and condemning voices—relief!

Jesus' sacrifice wasn't an easy thing, and this story reminds us of that, but it also reminds us that God himself is our ram of relief.

## Questions for Conversation:

1. What does it feel like when you're really tense? How does your body feel? How does your heart feel? How does it feel to experience relief?

2. What would it look like if you lived a life marked by "relief," where you believed that God cares for you and wants to be with you?

## Prayer:

Heavenly Father, the One Who Steps In,

We confess that we find ourselves tense for many reasons: bullies at school, bad grades, little or no work, challenging relationships, upsetting world events, poor health. It can be hard for us to believe that you want to give us relief. Remind us that through Jesus you have done everything that needs to be done so that we can flourish. In our tenseness, offer us your peace that we might fully breathe. We pray this in the name of Jesus the Son, who dwells with you and the Holy Spirit: one God, now and forever, amen.

**Day 6**

**Symbol:** Jacob's Ladder
**Reading:** Genesis 28:10-16 (Genesis 28:10-22*)
**Summary:** Today's symbol is Jacob's ladder. The ladder reminds us that God is always making a way to get close to us because he cares for us.

**Reflection:**
Ladders are for climbing. We all know that. You don't set up a ladder unless you need to go up it. You set it against the house to get to the gutter, or against a tree to climb up to your tree house, or you pull out the step stool to reach those high shelves. The same goes for a stairway. You don't build a stairway unless you're trying to get somewhere—typically, the second floor. This is all common sense. You go up, then you come down. Most of us do this daily.

But when Jacob sees a ladder or stairway or ziggurat (cool word—look that one up!) in his dream, he doesn't seize the opportunity to climb. We might expect him to, but he doesn't. The ladder he sees is not a path for him to ascend, but a way for God to show that he is coming down. It's a reversal!

Jacob wakes up and points out that the Lord is not simply waiting at the top of the staircase, but that he is "in this place" (v.16). The ladder is a reminder that the same God who hovered over the waters before the creation, the same God who can make a family as big as a sky full of stars, that same God is also with Jacob. And he's with us.

The ladder reminds us that God has always been coming close to us, as he came close to Jacob and as he ultimately came to live among us in the person of Jesus.

## Questions:

1. What would you do if you saw a ladder going into heaven? Would you climb it? Or would you ask God to come down?
2. What's your reaction to the idea that you don't have to "climb" to get close to God? Do you believe that's true?

## Prayer:

Descending Father,

We confess that we often try to climb our way to you. We try to be good children or good parents. We try to be good workers and good friends. But we never seem to be good enough. Thank you that you are always coming to us. Thank you that we don't earn our way into your presence by climbing fast enough or far enough, but that you simply welcome us because of Jesus. Help us to climb less and wait for you more. We pray this in the name of Jesus the Son, who dwells with you and the Holy Spirit: one God, now and forever, amen.

**Day 7**

**Symbol:** Joseph's Colored Coat
**Reading:** Genesis 37:1-4, 23-34; and Genesis 50:15-21 (Genesis 37 and Genesis 50:15-21*)
**Summary:** Today's symbol is Joseph's colored coat. The coat reminds us that God is at work when we are full of delight *and* when we are in great pain.

**Reflection:**

Have you ever felt an incredibly soft piece of fabric? You know, the kind of fabric you want to roll around in and make into a million blankets. Now imagine that this same fabric was dyed with colors that you don't even have names for: deep-sea-sky-blue, jungle-olive-chameleon-green, scarlet-sunset-blushing-red. And now imagine that you could wear this fabulous fabric as a coat. It fits just right and you know that you . . . look . . . GOOD.

We don't know what Joseph's "coat of many colors" looked like. It probably wasn't the softest fabric you've ever felt, and the colors might have been more familiar, but it was special nonetheless. It marked Joseph out as the favorite son, and when he was wearing it, he . . . looked . . . GOOD. The coat was a symbol of pride both for Joseph and for his father. But the coat would also become a symbol of pain. It would be the evidence Joseph's brothers falsely gave their father to "prove" that Joseph was dead.

In a broken world, it's a sad reality that those things dearest to us can also be the things that break our hearts most painfully, much like the coat.

But God doesn't leave things there. Joseph (not dead after all!) would rise to be the second-in-command in all of Egypt and would save the land from a famine. God used the pain of his brothers' jealousy and betrayal for good in amazing ways.

It's a grace, not a guarantee, but the two sides of the colored coat suggest that in the midst of our tears God invites us to look where he's stirring and beginning to work.

## Questions:

1. If you could wear one piece of clothing every day, what would it be?
2. How do you think you might look for God working even in seasons of pain or loss?

## Prayer:

Active Father,

It can be hard for us to believe that you are active in our lives when we are hurting. Thank you that you are patient with us and work with us so gently—not berating us, but inviting us to see you at work. Give us eyes to see you more clearly in our lives and help us experience you more fully. We pray this in the name of Jesus the Son, who dwells with you and the Holy Spirit: one God, now and forever, amen.

**Day 8**

**Symbol:** The Burning Bush
**Reading:** Exodus 3:1-15 (Exodus 3*)
**Summary:** Today's symbol is the burning bush. The burning bush reminds us that God is constant and faithful. He never runs out of fuel and is always there for us.

**Reflection:**
One of my favorite things about camping is waking up in the morning and trying to get the fire started again. I love digging through the ash with my "fire-poking stick" to see if there are any embers left. If I catch a glimpse of red, I put paper or pine needles or kindling around it and gently start to blow. With some patience and a little luck, the fire catches. But then, of course, it has to be fed. To get a roaring fire, you have to have plenty of fuel. Without fuel, fires go out.

No wonder Moses turned aside when he saw a bush burning with no sign of going out. Maybe he thought if he could find the source, his mornings of restarting the campfire would be over!

It's out of this fire that God speaks some deeply sacred words. He'd given wonderful promises before. He'd spoken words of grace to his people before. But here, in a fire without end, God speaks his own name. And his name is much like the unusual fire:

"I am who I am." As the fire in that moment was constant, so does God declare himself. "I am"—God is. He is constant.

Unlike the campfire that needs tending each morning, God is the ever-present, the ever-burning, the ever-with-us. He needs no fuel, no kindling, not even tending. He is just overwhelmingly, powerfully, for us and with us. God IS.

**Questions:**

1. What would you do if you found a fire that would burn forever?
2. In your life, are you trying to "tend to God" to make sure he's still for you? What does it mean to know that you don't have to do that?

**Prayer:**

Constant Father,

We try so many different ways to make things happen with you. We find ourselves thinking that we just need to do the right thing and you will be with us. Remind us that you are the great "I am"— that you are simply with us and for us, not because of what we do, but despite ourselves. Help us receive that truth as the deep grace that it is. We pray this in the name of Jesus the Son, who dwells with you and the Holy Spirit: one God, now and forever, amen.

**Day 9**

**Symbol:** The Tablets of the Law
**Reading:** Exodus 32:15-20, 34:1-9 (Deuteronomy 5:6-22*)
**Summary:** Today's symbol is the Tablets of the Law. The Tablets remind us that even when we break things or turn from God, he is willing to give us another chance.

**Reflection:**
My mom has the most beautiful cursive handwriting you have ever seen. When I was in elementary school, my teachers used to keep the notes she would write to get me out of school (on the rare occasion that happened).

When I think of the Tablets of the Law, I think of my Mom's handwriting. Here are two tablets, written on by the very hand of God. I think it is safe to assume that God's handwriting was perfectly legible and beautiful.

Moses comes down from the mountain with these beautiful tablets in hand and promptly smashes them to the ground in anger. The people of Israel, without Moses for only a short period of time, had decided to worship and dance before a fake god, a golden calf.

Perhaps we can understand Moses's frustration and anger, but I imagine ripping up one of my Mom's handwritten notes in front of her, and I know how things are going to go with Moses.

Broken tablets *and* idol worship—this will not end well. We might expect that to be the end of Israel's story with God, over before it began. But two chapters later, after some immediate consequences, there is a shift. The people are not shunned for all time.

In Exodus 34, two new stone tablets are cut and marked with the Law. God again identifies himself as "a gracious God, slow to anger, abounding in love and faithfulness" (Exodus 34:5). He has already started to prove it. In response to the people's foolishness and Moses's anger, God returns to his people and is willing to give them another chance.

## Questions:
1. Have you ever seen something beautiful fall apart? How did that make you feel?
2. What's your response to the idea that God's grace keeps coming back to us, even when we're disobedient or do something that could make God angry?

## Prayer:
Returning Father,
We admit that we often do bad things, sometimes bad things we know and sometimes bad things we're not even aware of. When we do these things, help us remember that, more than anything, you want to give us another chance. Forgive us for the bad things we do, and lead us more into your grace, love, and faithfulness. We pray this in the name of Jesus the Son, who dwells with you and the Holy Spirit: one God, now and forever, amen.

## Day 10

**Symbol:** A Cluster of Grapes
**Reading:** Numbers 13:1-2, 21-33
**Summary:** Today's symbol is a cluster of grapes. The grapes remind us that God wants abundantly good things for us and is with us in the challenges to get there.

**Reflection:**
Growing up, I remember watching an animated show featuring Winnie the Pooh. In one episode, some of the Hundred Acre Wood crew discovered a place called the Land of Milk and Honey. It had a volcano that erupted with honey, filling the streets with its cartoon deliciousness. To my young eyes, that was what abundance looked like.

The grapes in today's story probably had a similar effect on the Israelites. Imagine a cluster of grapes so weighty that it has to be carried on a pole by two men! As they walked into camp, we can guess that children's eyes widened, women whispered in surprise, and men openly gawked. The land that God had promised to give his people really was as good as they had hoped!

But big clusters of grapes are not come by easily. The Israelites looked at the size of the people in the land and declared they could never move into that neighborhood; the big guys would just kick them out. While God invites us to abundance, to lives marked by delight and joy in him, we often experience his abundance through challenges: things we have to give up, people we have to care for, habits we have to change.

The grapes of this story are not just a declaration that God had a land of milk and honey for his people. They are ultimately an invitation to trust that the God who brings us to the edge of abundance will be with us as we seek to experience that abundance in our lives. His faithfulness does not stop at easy things; he is with us in hard things as well.

**Questions:**
1. If someone made a feast with all your favorite foods, what foods would be on the table?
2. How has God been with you in the midst of some of the hard things in your life? How has this impacted what you think spiritual abundance looks like?

**Prayer:**
Abundant Father,
Thank you that you love to see abundance fill our lives. Forgive us for thinking this just means more stuff or better things. Help us see the abundance you invite us to as an abundance that comes from relationship with you. Thank you that you are with us on our journey, through our challenges and in our successes. We pray this in the name of Jesus the Son, who dwells with you and the Holy Spirit: one God, now and forever, amen.

**Day 11**

**Symbol:** A Head of Grain
**Reading:** Ruth 1:15-2:3, 4:9-11 (Ruth 1-4*)
**Summary:** Today's symbol is a head of grain. The grain reminds us that God works in our lives even when it seems like we have nothing to offer.

**Reflection:**
Remember the grapes from yesterday? The cluster that was so big that two men had to carry it on a pole? If the story of the Israelites looking at the land of milk and honey is about abundance, Ruth's story is about scraps.

The grain of today's story is not the best grain; it is the leftovers. The feet of a number of workers have trampled it. Yet, for all of the reasons we might turn our nose up at this grain, it also represents hope.

When the Israelites eventually move into the land of milk and honey (which they do!), we might expect the story of God's people to exhibit continual improvement. Things should just keep getting better, right?

But then, in a small book of the Bible we have this story—the story of Ruth. A story that's not marked by milk and honey, but by scraps and unwanted pieces of grain. For some reason, God seems to love working with scraps.

When all we have is leftovers, God likes to bring something new to life. He did it for Ruth.

Ruth's scrap-gathering mission led her to Boaz, who would become her husband. Together they would be the great-grandparents of King David, and ultimately ancestors of Jesus himself! From scraps to generations of kings.

It does not always happen that way for us, but a head of grain is a good reminder that when we don't have a lot, that might just be when God's eyes start to twinkle, he rolls up his sleeves, and he goes excitedly to work.

## Questions:

1. Imagine someone gave you a bunch of leftovers and asked you to make a delicious meal for someone special. How would you respond?
2. How might God's resourcefulness and willingness to work with scraps be a comfort to you?

## Prayer:

Resourceful Father,

Thank you that when we seem to have nothing to offer, you are ready to work. Remind us that we don't have to bring anything more than ourselves for you to love and receive us. Forgive us for the ways we try to make our own scraps look good instead of relying on you to transform them into something beautiful. We pray this in the name of Jesus the Son, who dwells with you and the Holy Spirit: one God, now and forever, amen.

**Day 12**

**Symbol:** Samuel's Oil
**Reading:** 1 Samuel 16:1-13
**Summary:** Today's symbol is Samuel's oil. The oil reminds us that God's call on our lives fills and covers every part of us, inviting us to belong to him.

**Reflection:**
Have you ever gotten vegetable oil on your hands? Or have you had a really greasy burger and fries? At the end of that meal, a napkin is not going to work well enough. You can try to get the grease off your fingers, but it will spread. Running water and soap seems to be the only real solution. Oil is slippery and messy. It is also expansive.

God's calling can be similar. We see it in the story of Samuel, a prophet of God, anointing David, the future king of Israel. With just a little oil poured over David's head, his life is changed. Like the grease after fast food, God's call spreads throughout his life, finding all the cracks and inviting him from life in the pasture to life in the palace.

God's call to us does not usually include oil today, but it is still just as immersive and expansive. It fills our lives. It seeps into our skin and gets to our deepest places.

In the New Testament, Christians are described as God's anointed people (1 John 2:27), people who have been covered in the oil of his calling. The only requirement on our part is that we listen. It is a life-changing call and it is secure in the deep promise that this anointing does not just call us to do or be or become something. It calls us to a new identity. Like David was called from being a shepherd to a king, God's call invites us to have our lives transformed by his invitation to belong to him.

**Questions:**
1. If you could be covered in any kind of liquid, which would you pick? Why?
2. Do you think that God's calling to belong to him can really be a part of every aspect of our lives? What might it look like if this was true?

**Prayer:**
Calling Father,
Thank you that your call to us does not ask us to be or become or do more good things. Thank you that your call is simply an invitation to receive your grace and belong to you. As we hear your call more clearly, help us experience our belonging in every aspect of our lives. We pray this in the name of Jesus the Son, who dwells with you and the Holy Spirit: one God, now and forever, amen.

**Day 13**

**Symbol:** The Sling
**Reading:** 1 Samuel 17:3-11, 32-50 (1 Samuel 17*)
**Summary:** Today's symbol is the sling. The sling reminds us that sometimes God works best through the familiar practices and day-to-day experiences of our lives.

**Reflection:**
The sword in the stone is an old British legend. The legend held that only the rightful king of England could withdraw a sword that was stuck fast in a large rock. When that king placed his hands on the sword, it would slide out, identifying England's true king. A sword for a king. The weapon fit the person.

By contrast, a sling is not quite as intimidating. A sling seems more like a toy than something people wear into battle. It is the weapon of cartoons and joke stores. But in today's story, it fits.

David had tried the alternatives—Saul's sword and armor, finely made—but David opted to rely on what he was used to: a staff, a sling, and trusting that God would protect and deliver his people. It was his use of something familiar that led to his success against Goliath.

The familiar can sometimes be boring to us, especially when it comes to how we approach God. A new way to pray, a new devotion to read, a new song to sing, or a new family practice might excite us. Sometimes we can want novelty at the expense of practices that have worked over and over. Sometimes we want the king's armor when we should pick up the familiar sling.

David's life had worn grooves of familiarity into his experience of God; he had practiced trusting God over and over. The familiar practices of our lives might also lead us more deeply into trusting God.

**Questions:**
1. Do you do things regularly to make you feel close to God? Pray? Read the Bible? Talk about God? Do you have a favorite practice?
2. What's a spiritual practice that you used to do that you stopped doing? Do you think it might be worth trying again?

**Prayer:**
Heavenly Father, God of Each Day,
Thank you that you do not require us to put on a show or do something flashy each day. Thank you that you meet us in our simple acts of faithfulness and that even when we are inconsistent, you still wait for us, wanting to be with us. Help us to not be distracted by new things, but to be drawn to you above all. We pray this in the name of Jesus the Son, who dwells with you and the Holy Spirit: one God, now and forever, amen.

**Day 14**

**Symbol:** A Scale
**Reading:** 1 Kings 3:5-14
**Summary:** Today's symbol is a scale. The scale reminds us that God is a God of justice, but also that he generously stacks things in our favor because of his grace.

**Reflection:**
Scales are all about balance. You put something on one side and something else on another and if they weigh the same, the two sides rest at the same height. A scale is a symbol of balance and, with balance, wisdom.

The scale is a fitting symbol when it comes to Solomon, the son of David (the beat-Goliath-with-the-familiar-sling guy). That's because Solomon is portrayed in the Bible as the wisest king who ever lived.

What is interesting is that the scale does not seem to be as fitting a symbol for God. God is certainly wise and cares about justice. Yet sometimes it seems like God is not in the balance business. We see it in the stories we have encountered so far. Abraham's family is not just large; his descendants are like a sky full of stars. The land that God sends his people to is not just okay; it is flowing with milk and honey and *huge* clusters of grapes. When Solomon asks God for wisdom, he receives not only wisdom, but also wealth and honor such that he will have no equal among kings (v.13).

We sometimes think that the path to God is marked by balance. If we can outweigh the bad things we do with good things, we will be set. But God laughs at balance. Instead he starts loading one side of the scale with grace—grace so rich and wonderful and weighty that the scale will always be tipped.

That is just how God is; he tips the scale like he did for Solomon, points, and says, "This is for you."

## Questions:

1. Has something good ever happened to you that felt unfair? What was it?

2. Do you think of God as a fair God or as a God who tips the scale in your favor? What would it look like if you believed God was for you?

## Prayer:

Generous Father,

Forgive us for thinking we can balance the things we do wrong with good things, ignoring you completely. Thank you that you are more interested in grace than balance. We ask that you would unbalance our lives with your grace, that we might share it with those around us. We pray this in the name of Jesus the Son, who dwells with you and the Holy Spirit: one God, now and forever, amen.

**Day 15**

**Symbol:** Fire on the Altar
**Reading:** 1 Kings 18:16-39 (1 Kings 18:16-46*)
**Summary:** Today's symbol is fire on the altar. The fire reminds us that God wants to reveal himself to us because he cares deeply for us.

**Reflection:**
I remember as a child sitting in the back seat of the car as our family drove through a controlled burn. A controlled burn is a fire that is started on purpose to make sure an area does not grow too prone to wildfires. As we drove through, with dying embers on the left and right, it was *hot*. The kind of hot that goes right through the glass of a car window and scalds your cheeks. That kind of heat is like an exclamation point. It is as if the fire is saying, "Here I am!"

As I read about Elijah's experience, I imagine his cheeks burned as well. God sends a fire that burns the very stones of the altar. The water that had covered the whole thing goes up in a puff of steam. God does not just say, "Here I am," God yells it!

Exclamation point experiences are great. They are so great that a lot of us try to force them to happen. When we do, we sometimes end up more like the prophets of Baal, dancing and yelling and begging, than like Elijah.

God wants to make himself known, but he does not always do it with an exclamation point. The simplicity of Elijah's prayer might be a help to us when God is quieter. His prayer reminds us that we do not have to dance and yell; we can simply ask for God to make himself known because God cares for us and wants us to know him. And who knows? Maybe he will show up with fire.

**Questions:**
1. Have you ever had an "exclamation point experience" of God?
2. Do you ever find yourself just waiting for the next big spiritual experience? How might you join Elijah's prayer regardless of whether you have an amazing experience like that?

**Prayer:**
Revealing Father,
We confess that sometimes we struggle to believe that you want us to know you. We get preoccupied with performing or doing things to make you like us. Thank you that you do not hide yourself from us or require that we dance to get your attention, but that you desire to reveal yourself to us so that we might know you. We pray this in the name of Jesus the Son, who dwells with you and the Holy Spirit: one God, now and forever, amen.

**Day 16**

**Symbol:** Isaiah's Scroll
**Reading:** Isaiah 9:2-7 (Isaiah 8:19-9:7*)
**Summary:** Today's symbol is Isaiah's scroll. The scroll reminds us that even in hard times, God offers us words of hope that can transform our lives.

**Reflection:**

Words have a special kind of power. A word of kindness can make our day, and a cruel playground nickname can hurt us for years. Some words have a short lifetime, but some words stay with us: words spoken with spite, words spoken with love, words of anger, words of hope. Some words are so meaningful that we find ways to record them so we can keep them and hold them close.

Isaiah's words were like that. They were recorded on scrolls, but many people would have also committed them to memory, pulling the words inside of them. But there is another property of words, one we might remember from the beginning of this story we have been exploring: words have the power to *create*.

In today's reading, Isaiah offers words of hope. Isaiah delivered many words, including some of judgment or condemnation. The words of Isaiah 9, however, are different. They are creative words—words that root themselves deep inside and create hope. We can imagine the Israelites holding onto words like "justice" and "righteousness," "Wonderful Counselor" and "Prince of Peace," letting them soak into their hearts. As Isaiah communicates these ideas, the words start to do their work.

Part of following the biblical story toward Jesus is recognizing the stirring of these words in our hearts. In today's reading, we again find God whispering unexpected hope into being. We are not much different than the Israelites; we need words of hope as well. Perhaps we can hear these words about Jesus, spoken before he was ever born, as words to create hope in us today.

**Questions:**
1. What is one of your favorite ideas about God? Can you say it in a single word?
2. If there was a "creating word" you needed to hear from God, what might it be? Do you believe that God wants to speak that to you?

**Prayer:**
Speaking Father,
Thank you that your words are not empty but are creative, doing something in us. We ask that you would help us hear and receive your words, that we might become people of hope and faith. We pray this in the name of Jesus the Son, who dwells with you and the Holy Spirit: one God, now and forever, amen.

## Day 17

**Symbol:** Esther's Crown
**Reading:** Esther 4:11-17, 8:5-10
**Summary:** Today's symbol is Esther's crown. Her crown reminds us that sometimes God picks unexpected people, or people who do not seem to "fit," to do his work.

### Reflection:

Crowns are not common things in our world. However, children know what is going on with crowns. They put on a tiara and suddenly they are lords and masters of all they survey. You will never receive such commanding instruction as when a four-year-old has donned this powerful headgear. In the case of make believe, it is delightful and sometimes even funny, but in the Old Testament, the crown really mattered.

We have seen kings before in our story. Samuel's oil anointed David to be king. Elijah's fiery altar was a response to a bad king. Even Isaiah's words from yesterday talked about a prince of peace. However, we see far fewer queens taking center stage. So when we get to Esther's story we might be lulled into thinking that she does not matter much. She is a woman, and in biblical times women did not often seem to have the crown or power. Here, though, the story takes a turn. Esther's unexpected rise meets unexpected responsibility, which turns into unexpected success.

Queen Esther was able to guide the king to spare her people, the Jews, in a time when they were far from home. That's true power. Like many of God's actions in Scripture, this is not how we would expect it to happen or who we would expect to do it. But Esther rose to the occasion, and the crown ended up being a perfect fit.

What unexpected things might God think you are a perfect fit for?

## Questions:
1. If you were king or queen for a day, what would you do?
2. Are there people in your life that you think of as lacking significance? How might your view change if you thought God wanted to do something exciting with or through those people?

## Prayer:
Unexpected Father,
Thank you that you work with us, even when it seems to us like we do not fit. We confess that sometimes we think we know how you should act or what you should do. Help us to be open to the unexpected things you want us to do, or the unexpected people you invite us to care for. We pray this in the name of Jesus the Son, who dwells with you and the Holy Spirit: one God, now and forever, amen.

**Day 18**

**Symbol:** A Lion
**Reading:** Daniel 6:16-23 (Daniel 6:1-23*)
**Summary:** Today's symbol is a lion. The lion reminds us that we can trust God even in situations that might scare or intimidate us.

### Reflection:

One Christmas, our family visited a local zoo. We saw all sorts of animals: monkeys and a leopard, reptiles and wolves. Then we came to the lion enclosure. There was the lion, a foot away on the other side of the glass, walking back and forth. I think we were all doing the same mental calculations: how much glass could a lion break through if it really wanted to eat us?

It's hard to imagine what it was like for Daniel to be in the lion's den without the benefit of zoo-approved glass. Yet the story does not tell us anything about Daniel's reaction. All we see is a faith-filled Daniel declaring at daybreak that God kept him safe. It's a remarkable story not just because of the miracle, but also because of Daniel's response.

For most of us, fear trumps faith. When the fearful voice in the back of our minds starts speaking up, it goes from a whisper to a yell in a second. When we're faced with something intimidating, our instinct is to be afraid, not to turn to God in trust.

Daniel's story does not provide a formula for protection, nor does it guarantee that the things we fear will not happen. What it offers us is a different posture. Daniel's story reminds us that God is a God who can be trusted. In the fearful circumstances of our own lives, he can be relied on. The things we are afraid of will not necessarily go away, but we can be confident that God is with us in the midst of them.

**Questions:**
1. What is something you are afraid of?
2. What do you think it looks like to trust God in scary or intimidating situations? What are the "lions" in your own life?

**Prayer:**
Trustworthy Father,
We admit that there are lots of things we are afraid of. Thank you that in the midst of our fears, you are with us. Help us to trust you more in the moments when we are intimidated or overwhelmed, that we might be marked by faith and not fear. We pray this in the name of Jesus the Son, who dwells with you and the Holy Spirit: one God, now and forever, amen.

**Day 19**

**Symbol:** The Great Fish
**Reading:** Jonah 1:1-2:1, 2:10-3:5 (Jonah 1-4*)
**Summary:** Today's symbol is the great fish. The fish reminds us that God will go to great lengths to tell us he loves us and to save us from our brokenness.

**Reflection:**

One of my favorite things about the Monterey Bay Aquarium is the Open Sea Exhibit. There, you look through a 90-foot tall window at tuna and sardines swimming and darting around. The fish seem to change direction so quickly, yet somehow they stay together. There is a dancing quality about the whole thing. Ultimately though, a fish's purpose is simple: get food, and avoid scary things.

When we think about the great fish of Jonah's experience, it is surprising that such a simple creature would play such a purposeful role. Fish are not usually a means of transportation for us, nor are they typically instruments of God.

However, Jonah's story reminds us that God deeply cares for people and will do whatever he can to save them.

Jonah is not really at the heart of this story, though. Rather, at the heart of this whole story is a people that God wanted to save— the people of Nineveh.

It was a success story on that front. The people of Nineveh heard that they were not acting like God wanted them to, and they took action. They mourned and fasted and asked for God's forgiveness.

And God gave it.

That might seem like a weighty purpose for a fish, but God is always reaching out to us, calling us to himself, and reminding us that he loves us. He loves us so deeply that even a fish can find purpose in order to save people God cares about.

**Questions:**

1. What is something crazy you might do to tell someone you loved them?

2. Do you think God goes to extreme lengths to communicate his love and care for you in your own life? What do you think that looks like?

**Prayer:**

Loving Father,

Thank you for Jesus and the way he showed us the lengths to which you will go to demonstrate your love. Remind us of your love for us when we doubt it. Help us be people who show that same love to those around us. We pray this in the name of Jesus the Son, who dwells with you and the Holy Spirit: one God, now and forever, amen.

**Day 20**

**Symbol:** The Jesse Tree
**Reading:** Isaiah 11:1-11 (Isaiah 11*)
**Summary:** Today's symbol is the Jesse Tree. The Jesse Tree reminds us that God can bring new life and hope out of even the most despairing of situations.

**Reflection:**
I remember going to visit my grandparents' house when I was around four years old. Along part of the drive was a series of tall trees lined up in row after row. I found out later that it was not a natural forest. It had been grown to be chopped down, to provide wood for buildings and paper and other materials. There was something sad about that almost-forest; I knew that one day it would just be row upon row of stumps. Stumps do not grow back.

The people of Israel may have felt that way. Our reading reminds us that when Isaiah shared these words, there was only a remnant of Israel left, and they were scattered all over the known world. They were a stump, a once-great nation brought to nothing. But then Isaiah 11 starts.

You can hear the music swell with the words "a shoot will come up from the stump of Jesse" (v. 1). Jesse was the father of King David, and here, where all looks hopeless, Isaiah suggests that there might be one coming who follows in the same line. From the despair of a scattered people comes One upon whom the Spirit of the Lord rests and who is unlike anybody this world has seen.

Sometimes our own lives can feel like stumps. Maybe we lost a friend, or we got picked on at school, or we recently lost a job. Isaiah's words speak to us too. God does not leave us with stumps; he longs to bring new life to us. Ultimately, he does that through Jesus. Here on Day 20 of the Jesse Tree, we are getting closer and closer to that good news.

**Questions:**
1. What's one thing that you wish you could change about the world?
2. Where can you see "green shoots" in your life or in the world around you—signs that God is beginning to work or that people are living more like Jesus?

**Prayer:**
Father of Hope,
You are with us even when we want to despair, and when the world feels too scary or overwhelming. Thank you that your promise to bring new life leads us to hope. We ask that you would fill our lives with "green shoots" so that those areas of our lives that are hurting and broken may be renewed. We pray this in the name of Jesus the Son, who dwells with you and the Holy Spirit: one God, now and forever, amen.

**Day 21**

**Symbol:** The Angel
**Reading:** Luke 1:5-17 (Luke 1:5-25*)
**Summary:** Today's symbol is an angel. The angel reminds us that sometimes God appears to us in surprising ways, but we are always invited to expect God to show up.

**Reflection:**
Have you ever wondered what an angel looks like? For all the mention of them in the Bible, we only have some fleeting descriptions. In some places they are depicted as having six wings; in other places it sounds like they might look like a regular person. Whatever they look like, they often evoke a common response: awe and fear. Angels always seem to be saying things like "do not be afraid"; there is something about them that wows us.

Zechariah responded in the same way, but there was something different about his reaction. He was afraid, yes, but he was also startled. Startled? This seems strange, because if ever there was a place that Zechariah should have expected to encounter an angel, it was there in the very heart of God's Temple. But Zechariah did not expect to see an angel. He did not expect to encounter the message of God even there, in that place.

If we are being honest, we would probably be startled too. God's work often takes us completely by surprise. Thankfully, God is patient with us when he startles us. Even though Zechariah was startled and afraid, God's word to him was still true: he and Elizabeth were going to have a son.

As we come closer to the story of the birth of Jesus, it is helpful to remember that we are invited to expect God to show up—not just in the heart of the Temple, but all around us, because God loves to take us by surprise.

**Questions:**
1. What is the best surprise that ever happened to you? What made it a good surprise rather than a bad surprise?
2. What would your life look like if you expected God to show up and reveal himself to you each day? What shape do you think that would take?

**Prayer:**
Surprising Father,
We confess that too often we do not expect you to be present in our lives. We keep our eyes shut and miss the way you are working. Help us to be aware of the ways, both big and small, that you are at work in our lives, and help us to delight in the ways you might surprise us. We pray this in the name of Jesus the Son, who dwells with you and the Holy Spirit: one God, now and forever, amen.

**Day 22**

**Symbol:** A Heart
**Reading:** Luke 1:26-38 (Luke 1:26-56\*)
**Summary:** Today's symbol is a heart. The heart reminds us that, like Mary, we want to allow God's Word to fill our hearts and renew us.

**Reflection:**
Have you ever considered that your heart has a landscape? Not your physical heart, but the heart that contains all of your feelings and thoughts, the core part of you. Macarius, an Egyptian Christian monk, described the heart as containing dragons, lions, and poisonous beasts. He saw the heart as having uneven roads and cliffs. He also described the heart as containing the treasures of grace, light, and the kingdom of God.

Macarius used images to explain that our hearts are often divided. We desire good things and we desire bad things. We have been mixed up from the day our ancient ancestors chose to disobey God. Maybe your dragon is being mean to your friend, or your lion is cheating on taxes. Maybe your poisonous beast is a tongue that is a little too quick to speak. But our heart is not just a place for dragons, it is also a space that God wants to enter, and when he does, the landscape gets thoroughly rearranged.

That is Mary's experience in today's story. She receives amazing (and shocking!) news from God, and rather than refuse it, she receives it. We can imagine the landscape of her heart being filled with light and the dragons and lions fleeing as God's Word made his home within her.

Mary's faithful hearing of God's Word is a model for all of us, but hearing is not quite enough. With Mary, we want to allow God's Word to penetrate to our inner landscape so that God might bring light and life and all good things into our hearts.

**Questions:**
1. If you were describing the landscape of your heart, what would be there? Castles? A network of underground tunnels? A large ocean?
2. How might this image of our hearts having a landscape be helpful in understanding our internal struggles? Can you imagine God being the most prominent part of the landscape of your heart? What would that look like?

**Prayer:**
Father of Light and Life,
Thank you that, because of your grace, you see what our hearts look like and still long to dwell in us. We confess that our hearts are often dangerous places, and we get lost in them. We ask that you would bring light and life to the landscape of our heart. We pray this in the name of Jesus the Son, who dwells with you and the Holy Spirit: one God, now and forever, amen.

**Day 23**

**Symbol:** A Carpenter's Tools
**Reading:** Matthew 1:18-25
**Summary:** Today's symbol is a carpenter's tools. The tools remind us that as much as we might like care and precision, God's message comes to us and invites us to an often-uncomfortable and unfamiliar adventure.

**Reflection:**

My grandfather loves carpentry. For as long as I can remember, he always had a shed in the backyard that housed his table saws, hand saws, workbenches, and a ton of other tools. He made beautiful pieces of furniture that fit together perfectly. They were a reminder of the care and precision that carpentry requires.

Joseph was a carpenter himself. Care and precision were not just tools of his trade, they marked his life. He had planned on marrying Mary, but when things did not work out quite as planned, he chose to act carefully. He would divorce her quietly so as to protect her, knowing that things would already be hard for a single mother.

Care and precision seem like godly qualities. But the angel of the Lord does not advocate care and precision. Instead the angel directs Joseph to engage with the messiness of Mary's life and to take on Jesus as his own son so that Jesus can do the messy work of saving his people from their sins. Joseph was launched onto this trajectory; there was no time to "measure twice, cut once." But he, like we saw Mary do, received God's message and put it into action.

Sometimes living in response to God's message is not familiar. If we are careful and precise people, living God's way sometimes calls us to have the spontaneity of a tornado. If we are wild and unpredictable, living God's way sometimes looks like pausing and gathering ourselves to live more deliberately. The key is responding to and embracing God's message even when it runs counter to our inclinations.

## Questions:

1. Are you more careful or more wild? Which one do you think is better?
2. Can you think of a time when you felt that God's message for you was something uncomfortable? How did you deal with it? How should you have dealt with it?

## Prayer:

Adventurous Father,
You invite us to the unfamiliar, to step out of our comfort zone. We confess that while for some of us that is exciting, for others that feels scary. Bring comfort to us and give us the courage to step into the adventure you call us on. We pray this in the name of Jesus the Son, who dwells with you and the Holy Spirit: one God, now and forever, amen.

**Day 24**

**Symbol:** The Manger
**Reading:** Luke 2:1-20
**Summary:** Today's symbol is the manger. The manger reminds us that God's abundant presence shows up in unexpected places and is available to all of us.

**Reflection:**
We have been waiting for this day, haven't we? Ever since we read about the fruit and began to look towards God's plan to heal us. Ever since we got glimpses of how God wanted to come near and be with us. Ever since we heard Isaiah's words that from a dead stump would come a green shoot—a king like David. Here we are, at the culmination of all these stories.

And they all point to . . . a manger? A feeding trough for animals is the climax of God's plan? I wonder how the shepherds felt when they were told that the sign of the Messiah, the One anointed with God's calling, was a baby lying in a manger. Who puts a Savior in a feeding trough?

But this is what we have seen throughout God story: God works in unexpected ways. The giant is slain not with the king's sword, but with a familiar sling. A woman is crowned queen and saves her people. A scrap of leftover grain makes a foreigner the grandmother of King David.

But the manger is not just another surprise; it is something else entirely. The baby is not just a *sign* of God's presence, he *is* Immanuel, God With Us. This is the beginning of something new. God is not merely in the Temple or in our places of worship. He is here. With us. Abundantly and unexpectedly and available to any who would visit.

The Jesse Tree tells this story: the story of a God who keeps showing up with unexpected abundance so that he can be with us.

## Questions:

1. If you were one of the shepherds, do you think you would have believed that God showed up in a manger? Does that seem like something God would do?
2. Do you recognize the abundance of God when you see it?

## Prayer:

Gracious Father,

We confess that we do not deserve the grace you show us. Yet you continue to show up in our lives, unexpectedly and abundantly. Thank you for the gift of Jesus, who embodies who you are: a God of unexpected and abundant grace. We pray this in the name of Jesus the Son, who dwells with you and the Holy Spirit: one God, now and forever, amen.

Download a PDF of all 24 symbols
to hang on your tree

granitesprings.org/jessetree

57518874R00033

Made in the USA
San Bernardino, CA
21 November 2017